# Military Knife Fighting

© 1996 by Robert K. Spear

Published by Desert Publications
P.O. Box 1751
El Dorado, AR 71731-1751
501-862-2077

ISBN 0-87947-179-4
10 9 8 7 6 5 4 3 2 1
Printed in U. S. A.

Desert Publication is a division of
The DELTA GROUP, Ltd.
Direct all inquiries & orders to the above address.

# MILITARY KNIFE FIGHTING

You may never need to fight for your life with a knife, but... wouldn't it be nice to know how if you do!

by

## Robert K. Spear

**Desert Publications**
El Dorado, AR 71731-1751 U. S. A.

# ABOUT THE AUTHOR

A fifth-degree black belt, Mr. Spear is considered an American pioneer in the Korean street fighting art of Hapkido. In 1975, he was the first American in Korea to attain a third-degree black belt and instructor's certification with the Korea Hapkido Association. He is now the chairman of the United States Hapkido Federation's Board of Examiners. He also oversees the Hapkido aspects of the Midori Yama Budokai Jujitsu Association.

A former U.S. Army Intelligence officer, Mr. Spear has taught combat fighting and self-defense to soldiers, security forces, and civilians throughout Europe, the U.S., and Korea since 1974.

An internationally recognized martial arts theorist and author, Mr. Spear has presented papers on martial art research to such august bodies as the 1984 and 1988 Olympic Scientific Congresses. He has been published in international scientific academic journals and in such magazines as Soldier of Fortune and American Survival Guide. His previous books include:
- Survival on the Battlefield
- Hapkido: The Integrated Fighting Art
- Surviving Hostage Situations (coauthor)
- Close-Quarters Combat For Police and Security Forces

Mr. Spear is a career civil servant for the U.S. Army. He presently writes the Deception Operations concepts for the Army's Combined Arms Command at Ft. Leavenworth, KS.

# TABLE OF CONTENTS

# FOREWORD

If you received this book as part of your purchase of a Field Fighter Combat Knife, congratulations!  You now own a wonderful fighting weapon which was human engineered specifically for fighting yet will also double as an excellent general purpose camping or hunting knife.  This manual was written to show you how to get the best performance out of yourself and your weapon.

If you bought this book separately from the knife, don t worry.  The principles also apply to most other combat knifes and will provide you with an excellent approach to knife fighting.  If you would like to purchase your own Field Fighter Combat Knife, queries should be sent to:

**Ek Knives**
**601 N. Lombardi St.**
**Richmond, VA  23220**
**1-800-468-5575**

# MILITARY KNIFE FIGHTING

There are many books written about fighting. Some are good, some aren't. Those written specifically for knife fighting represent the same wide variety of quality. None, however, address the special needs of military and para-military personnel. This book has been written to fill this glaring gap. The techniques contained herein have been designed to safeguard the knifefighter while providing the tools to take an opponent out as quickly as possible. The techniques are easily taught to a large class of students (which is important for military training requirements). The fighting style suggested is not fancy or flashy, but it is effective.

With so many hucksters tauting their books on fighting, a discerning reader might question the validity of the materiel presented. This author spoke with a man once who claimed the writer of a very popular book on how to use poisons to kill was only eighteen-years-old when he wrote it. One can't help but wonder what kind of credentials and experience the lad had. Perhaps he should have submitted his name to the Guiness Book of Records as the world's youngest assassin.

So, OK, Mr. Spear, put your money where your mouth is! What makes you an expert on knife fighting? How many people have you maimed or killed? Which street gang did you join? Where have you served prison time? To answer these questions, I must tell you what I am and what I am not.

# WHAT I'M NOT

First, I can't claim to be a macho, studly super athlete anymore. Although I used to be fit, strong, and fast, those days are behind me now. Today I am on the higher side of my forties. I've lost a lot of my hair. My knees, ankle, and lower spine are crippled by deteriorating cartilage and osteo-arthritis. I've had four operations on my left knee, two on my right ankle, and one on my right knee. Since I can no longer run, kick, or even walk very far, my weight has climbed alarmingly. Although my reactions are still quick, my body certainly isn't. Pain has been my constant companion since 1978, but I still manage to function, and I still teach my beloved Hapkido classes. If nothing else, I've learned how to put pain on the shelf, out of the way.

I was never a member of a street gang in the barrio or ghetto. I grew up in a lower-middle class neighborhood in Lafayette, Indiana (which seemed at the time to be the most boring community in the world). We kids fought for fun, for something to do. In our quest for excitement, my friends and I got into some fairly exotic stuff. Knife throwing became a passion. We used to play the game, "stretchem". Two guys would stand face-to-face, toe-to-toe. They would take turns throwing a knife so it stuck in the ground within 6-12 inches of the other guy's foot. If it didn't stick, you lost your turn. Wherever it stuck, the other player had to move his foot over to touch the knife, reach down to pull it out, and take his turn at throwing. The

3

game ended when one player couldn't stretch any further; or, when the knife accidently got stuck in a player's foot, as happened to me one time.

We also thought it a challenge to play catch with knives. We would stand about 25 to 50 feet apart and underhand a hunting knife back and forth to one another. The idea was to catch it without getting cut or stuck. This took a keen eye and a sense of timing.

Our variety of play was significantly improved when Captain Kingsberry moved in across the street. An Air Force ROTC instructor at Purdue University, he taught us how to fence with the saber and how to fight with the quarter-staff. He had learned these ancient skills at West Point before the Air Force had its own Academy.

We would go out into the woods, cut saplings, and whale away at one another for hours. The concept of protective gear, gloves, padding, etc., never even entered our minds. Instead, we relied on our own reactions and self-control to keep the injury rate down.

When I was ten, another neighbor taught us how to braid bullwhips and how to crack them properly. Using a cloth shoelace "cracker" tied onto the end of the whip, we would execute front, rear, "S", and circular cracks which could be heard blocks away. We then tied rawhide bootlaces on instead of the cloth ones. With these cutting crackers, we used our whips to cut water melons in two and to cut cigarettes out of each other's mouth.

# FOREWORD

It wasn't long before this escalated into "Lash LaRou" type whip fights. I still bear scars on my arms from whip cuts.

Later on, we cut TV antennas up to make blow guns. We used to insert the "eye" end of a sewing needle into the end of a kitchen match. Then we wrapped cotton around the match until it just fit freely into the tube. We were then ready to conduct our own style of drive-by shootings— a dart to the butt of a guy from another neighborhood as we peddled by.

In all, I had a normal boyhood filled with all the usual crazy, aggressive, daredevil fun which male adolescents of the 50s and 60s were prone to have.

The only time I've been behind bars was as the result of teaching dozens of college business courses for a couple of community colleges in three of Leavenworth, Kansas' five prisons. Many convicts and guards have shared war stories with me about shanks, shanking, and the cult of prison assassins; however, I never had the misfortune of participating in such an event myself (although, I once had a World War I French bayonet stuck through my arm in a mock battle at the age of fourteen.)

For three years of enlisted service, ten commissioned service, and over ten years of civil service with the Army, I never marched into battle, fired a shot in anger, or slit a sentry's gullet. My duties always revolved around electronic warfare and signals intelligence. Still, I identified very closely with the special ops mentality. In fact, I ran a semi-covert operation for about a year; however, there was no immediate risk to myself or my men.

# WHAT I AM

So, what makes me qualified to write a book on military knife fighting? In addition to all the crazy things I did in my youth, I wrestled all through Junior High and High School. During my freshman year at Indiana University, I fought 34 intramural fencing matches and lost only one.

I played judo in college and in my early Army years, to include training in Germany's Olympic training center in Frankfurt with instructors who had studied at the Kodokan Judo University in Tokyo.

In Korea, I immersed myself in the study of Hapkido for almost three years— sometimes practicing 4-5 hours per day, four days a week. This was where all my previous combative experiences and skills came together. Hapkido was such a multi-faceted art. Although there are no formal katas, Hapkido is considered one of the most complex of the martial arts with literally thousands of technique combinations. Free sparring was full go with no protective equipment. Weapons such as short fighting sticks, walking canes, Bo staff, bamboo kendo swords, ropes, and the like were also used. The reflexes and control I had gained in my childhood experiences came into play constantly in these sessions.

Hapkido is a very smooth, flowing type of art. It uses both soft and hard, circular and straight-line techniques. It seemed so natural to couple its flow with my love of bladed weapons.

Back in the early 1970's, when Palladin Press was still kind of an underground, word-of-mouth resource, I acquired a copy of Bob Loveless' knife fighting book. Much of what he taught made considerabe more sense than all the works I had seen previous to that time. Using his conservative fighting style as a foundation, I added the theories and flow of Hapkido stick fighting.

For thousands of hours over the years, my students and I have experimented with many knife fighting styles. Shunning rubber knives as too soft and unrealistic, we used hardwood tanto practice knives. These bruise and scrape, but leave no permanent damage. They do hurt like heck, thus creating a healthy respect for the weapon and its use.

I might add, most of my students have been military intelligence analysts and operatives, military police bodyguards, and special operations troops. They came to me to receive the type of realistic personal combat training they craved but rarely saw in their military units.

Why did these highly intelligent, profes-sional soldiers come to me for additional instruction? What did a partially crippled, fat old man with no real-life combat experience have to offer? Perhaps the same thing that short, fat, old Angelo Dundee had to offer his world champion boxers.

One common theme in my life has been the the ability to analyze and integrate many factors into something useful. Many things contributed to this: involvement in an advanced science program in high school; six years as a professional musician, composing, arranging, and playing for bands and recording studios; military intelligence analysis training and experience; and the test and evaluation of highly complex electronic warfare systems. The mental skills required in all these endeavors are the same. In fact, I used these same tools to conduct martial art research since the early 1970's. As a martial art theorist, my goal has always been to take a fighting concept and determine its feasibility and application for the street or battlefield. My philosophy is similar to the Physicians' Hippocratic Oath (Never cause harm to a patient.): Never cause harm to a student by teaching an inadequate technique or approach.

The techniques portrayed in this manual are based on common sense. There are no guarantees because fight environments are too complex to predict consistently; however, the techniques have been designed to provide the best chance for successfully surviving and winning an edged weapon confrontation.

Remember this proverb my old Hapkido instructor, Major Song Ho Jin of the Korean

# FOREWORD

Marines, said: "Lots of sweat in the dojang (gym),
little blood (of your own) on the street!"

The author demonstrating a Hapkido flying front kick / inside crescent kick combination in Korea in 1975.

# CHAPTER 1

# THE BIRTH OF A FIGHTING KNIFE

It was September, 1990. Soldier of Fortune magazine was holding their fifteen anniversary SOF Convention at the Sahara Hotel in Las Vegas, Nevada. I had been back Stateside a little over a year, returning from Munich, Germany, where I had been working as a civil service technical advisor to the 66th Military Intelligence Brigade. While I had been stationed there, my first two books, **Survival on the Battlefield: A Handbook to Military Martial Arts** and **Hapkido: The Integrated Fighting Art**, had been published by Unique Publications out of Burbank, California. Although I had toured Europe, doing author signings for the Stars and Stripes bookstore system, nothing had been done to promote my books in the U.S.

Unique, a martial arts specialty house which

produces such magazines as Inside Kung Fu and Inside Karate magazines, just didn't have the familiarity with the military market which my books needed. Since I was doing the only real promoting anyway, I figured, "What the heck, I think I could probably do this." I returned from Munich to pick up my third book from the printer, **Surviving Hostage Situations**, written with Special Ops officer, Major Mike Moak, the first which I had published myself.

The SOF Convention was my first chance to make an appearance giving me good exposure to the people for whom I wrote my books. What a great time that week was! Many stopped by our table to buy our books, but more importantly, there was the chance to meet people who were interested in what I was doing and who proved it by giving my titles positive reviews over the next year: John Coleman, editor of SOF, Denny Hansen of SWAT magazine, and Scott Stoddard and Jim Bensen of American Survival Guide.

Another fortunate meeting was with Ernie Franco, a highly respected, West-Coast based hand-to-hand trainer who was giving seminars at the convention. Ernie was familiar with **Survival on the Battlefield** and liked it. He suggested I contact Greg Walker of Fighting Knives Magazine about writing for him.

One of the nice aspects of the show is the display area for all the vendors. What a toy collection! There were so many goodies: from machine guns to camo garb to knives, knives, and more knives. I felt especially drawn to the custom knife makers. Although there were many good ones at the show, one man's work was particularly interesting.

Don Mount, a security guard at one of the nuclear test sites near Las Vegas, had turned a knifemaking hobby into a significant sideline. Don's knives were distinctive. The designs were original and well executed. I was particularly impressed with one feature he incorporated on several of his creations. He soldered a male snap onto the knife guard and fastened the female portion to a leather sheath. Thus the knife had a positive fastening to the carrying sheath. Although it was not conveniently placed for my purposes, I felt it demonstrated he was innovative and willing to try something new.

After we became acquainted, I mentioned to Don that I had never seen an ideal fighting knife which could also be used for camping and field purposes as well. During my thirteen years of active duty, I had always carried a Gerber Mark II for fighting and any one of a number of hunting knives for field work. Don said, "If you have a particular design in mind, I'd be glad to make it for you." I gave Don a copy of **Survival on the Battlefield** and asked him to read the chapter on military knife fighting.

That night in my hotel room, I jotted down on a small hotel note pad a long laundry list of features I felt an ideal fighting knife should have. The next day I approached Don and handed him the list. He said, "I read your book last night and it makes good sense to me! This list does too. Let me draw out a design and you tell me if it's what you want."

A couple of weeks after the show, the first set of drawings arrived in the mail. After several minor alterations and some phone calls, I sent them back. Within a month, the first prototype arrived with four different guards and a couple of handles. Don fashioned the knife so it could be taken apart and several different combinations of parts could be interchanged. I had two or three different improvements to suggest and then shipped the set back. Don then produced four beautiful prototypes which I sent around to various magazine editors to see their reaction.

The prototype, shown in figure 1, represents the design criteria I had given Don Mount plus the adjustments we agreed on afterward:

• 440 stainless steel to insure ease of maintenance— just wash with dish detergent, wipe dry, and spray with a silicon-based spray, then wipe dry. It is also easier to sharpen 440 stainless than it is to sharpen some of the more exotic, harder grades of steel.

• Grey finish (the result of glass bead blasting) to cut down on reflectivity. A shiny blade is not desirable for military applications. It might reflect light at the wrong time.

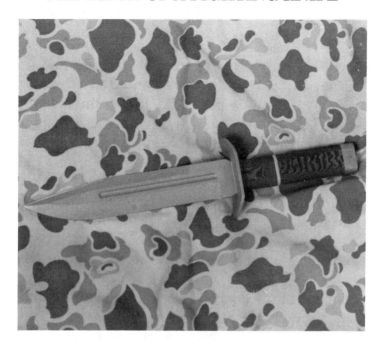

• Bottom edge sharpened on its full length for maximum cutting area.

• Top edge sharpened from the point back to the top of the blade to allow enough cutting surface for effective back-slashes, yet not too much so that the arm would be endangered when holding the knife in a ninja grip.

• The point begins to taper only over the last inch or so. This increases its strength similar to a Japanese Tanto design.

• Blade-catching angles at the base of the blade at the guard to allow the possibility of catching and twisting an opponent's weapon out of his hand.

• The giant brass guard— this feature, more than any other, makes this knife unique. The one feature I had always wanted on a fighting knife was adequate protection for my fingers and hand. I also wanted something to act as a stop for my thumb when I held the knife in a modified saber grip so my hand wouldn't slip down onto the blade if the knife point hit a bone or body armor. It's important that the guard be of a softer metal than steel so an opponent's blade might catch on it. The forward pointing brass guard, coupled with the blade-catching angles on the blade gives the best possibility of catching and twisting an opponent's knife out of his hand. The guard also brings the handle out away from the sheath just enough so that one can get a full grip on the knife as it is being drawn.

• The blade should be long enough to reach any vital organs. Its balance should be slightly forward to allow for easier slashing and hacking.

• There should be a blood groove to allow for easier extraction from a deeply stabbed body. Blood grooves help break the blade free from a natural vacuum or suction which will often takes place in these conditions.

• The knife should be heavy enough to provide strength and weight for both fighting and camp work.

• The longer than usual grip allows enough room for wide hands and pommel strikes.

# THE BIRTH OF A FIGHTING KNIFE

• The indented grip next to the guard allows the forefinger and thumb to rest beneath the top edge of the guard for their protection.

• In the knife picture, the handle is made out of roughened micarta. The production models of the Field Fighter series use a rubberized handle for a more positive grip, especially if it is wet or bloody.

These are the more important features of the Field Fighter Combat Knife series. Whether you have the 9.5-inch bladed Field Fighter I or the 6-inch bladed Field Fighter II, these features are incorporated. **Enjoy your new knife!**

For those who want a custom made knife of the highest quality, contact Don Mount. He's retired from the nuclear test site guarding business and is making knives full time in Missouri. Queries should be addressed to:

**Don Mount**
**800 Nellie Ave**
**Scott City, MO 63780**
**314-264-1287**

The author's Hapkido students in Munich, Germany performing plyometric exercises which develop explosive power in their arms and legs. The use of cutting-edge training methodologies is Mr. Spear's trademark.

# CHAPTER 2

# FIGHTING GRIPS AND STANCES

The correct manner in which to hold a knife depends on what you want to do with it. A perfectly good case could be made for holding a knife like a hammer in some situations; however, in others it might be terribly wrong. Much depends on whether the knife will be slashing or stabbing. Will it be used defensively or offensively or both? Are you walking into an uncertain situation under poor visibility, or is it a down-and-out knife brawl with everybody well aware of what's going on? What if you have a knife and your opponent has something else— such as a rifle and a bayonet, a club, or an entrenching tool. What if you're trying to take out a sentry as quietly as possible? What if you're faced with assassinating a guerilla leader in a densely packed urban environment and need to stick him and get away before anyone really notices anything's wrong?

# MILITARY KNIFE FIGHTING

Certain grips and fighting postures favor specific situations. In this chapter, we will address the strong and weak points of these different ways for holding your fighting knife and the situations for which they are best suited. The grips we will demonstrate are:

- Hammer Grip
- Ice Pick Grip
- Ninja Grip
- Saber Grip
- Modified Saber Grip

The stances we will cover are:

- The "Fencer"
- The "Classic" Military
- The "Hollywooder"
- The "Berserker"
- Ninja style
- Street Assassin
- Sentry Stalk

# GRIPS

# Hammer Grip

The Hammer Grip as shown in figure 1 is one of the strongest grips for thrusting a blade deep into an opponent's body cavity. If deep, low-line penetration is what you need, the hammer grip is a good choice. It is the grip favored in prison assassinations using the home made stabbing instrument called the "shank". It is not unusual for such an assassin to stab deeply into his victim's body ten, fifteen, even twenty times until all signs of resistance and life have disappeared.

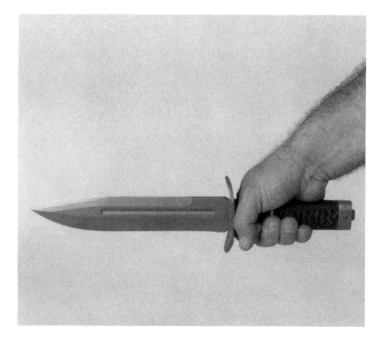

**Figure 1**

# MILITARY KNIFE FIGHTING

Its disadvantage is in the slash since it is too limited in directions of attack and too difficult to change the angle of attack in mid-movement or for follow-on attacks. Its strengths, a rigid wrist and strong hand-hold, cut back on its mobility.

It is extremely useful, however, when used as a grip for a pommel strike, as shown in figure 2. Used in this fashion, the pommel, if heavy, can easily crush an opponent's temple, nose, or the area in back of the skull where the neck vertebrae join with the skull. The pommel may also be used to temporarily numb muscle and nerve points if your intention is to take prisoners rather than to produce casualties. Figures 3 and 4 show a number of excellent target points for pommel attacks.

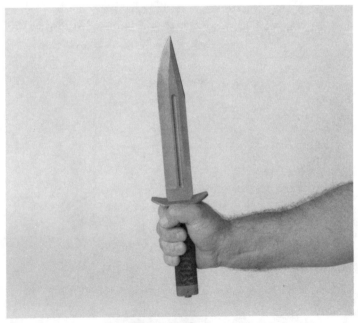

**Figure 2**

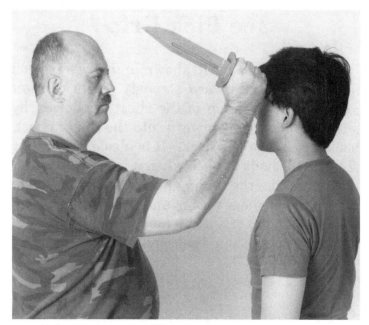

**Figure 3**

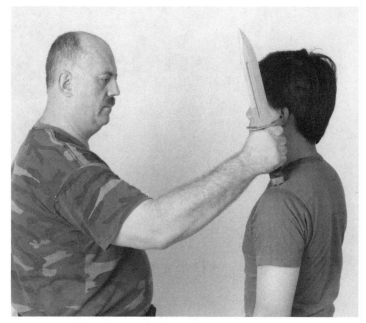

**Figure 4**

# Ice Pick Grip

The ice pick grip shown in figure 5 is good for stabbing downward strongly. One can get excellent penetration of the chest or thorax by stabbing deeply downward into the upper chest, back, or base of the neck. It is also excellent for stabs to the body or back when it is in a horizontal position. Like the hammer grip, the ice pick grip is meant for sheer power and deep penetration. Likewise, it has the same lack of mobility disadvantages for the same reasons.

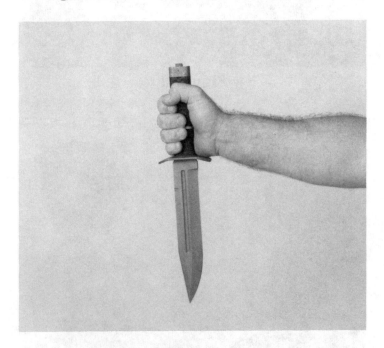

**Figure 5**

# Ninja Grip

Favored by many martial arts instructors, this grip is really a modified ice pick grip which allows the blade to rest against the underside of the forearm. This grip is best used for a surprize attack. It hides the blade from view (figure 6) and allows vertical (figure 7), horizontal (figure 8), and back (figure 9) slashes. The reverse of any slash is a stab on the return trip. Used with speed, power, and suddenness, this can be an effective fighting style. It does, however, have some limitations.

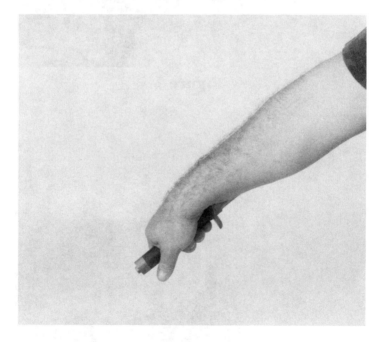

**Figure 6**

**Figure 7**

**Figure 8**

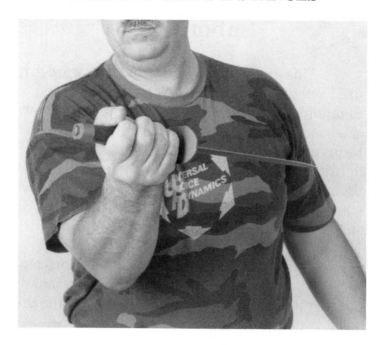

**Figure 9**

Once the opponent realizes that a "Ninja" style attack is happening, this grip's strength becomes its weakness. You don't have to keep track of the blade, just start slashing fingers and arms. The blade and point are back, relatively out of the way. Only the reverse stabs lead with the blade or point. This leaves the attacker's hand and arm rather vulnerable to counters. Of course, if you get surprized by <u>any</u> type of attack, oh well!

To change direction of a slash or stab with the "Ninja" grip, one must change the angle of the entire forearm. This does not provide ideal mobility for attacks or counters. When the whole forearm must move, the movement becomes much easier to read and to counter by an opponent.

**27**

# Saber Grip

This grip gets its name from the sword grip used on the knife's much larger cousin and is common among knowledgeable fighters. It allows good mobility of the wrist and a good reach in terms of range to the opposing fighter. Almost all fighting knives are set up for the saber grip in that their guards are designed to protect the fingers when the blade is in the vertical orientation as shown in figure 10.

It is a good grip with only two shortcomings— the vertical orientation of the blade makes it difficult to puncture through the rib cage and the wrist is not as completely free as it could be.

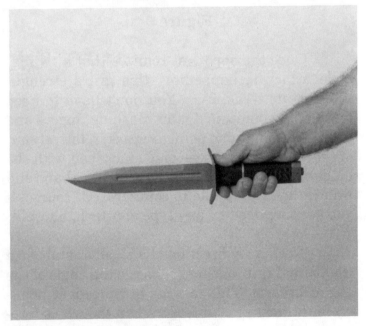

**Figure 10**

# Modified Saber Grip

This grip (figure 11) is the most versatile, allowing maximum freedom of movement for the wrist and a horizontal blade orientation for thrusts into the chest area. The blade is more likely to enter between ribs. Even if you hit a rib, it is more likely to split, allowing penetration into the chest cavity.

The issue of wrist mobility is extremely important when fast changing attacks, counter attacks, and blocking must be involved. The grip is strong and flexible. Most fighting knives, however, do not allow sufficient protection for one's

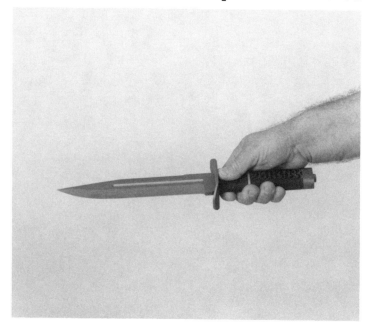

**Figure 11**

fingers, thumb, and hand when held in this position. Nor do they provide a stop for your thumb to prevent your hand from sliding down your own blade in case your point hits a bone or body armor. The Field Fighter knives, however, have been designed to allow maximum protection for the hand regardless of what grip is used. That is why the guards are so large and extend around the sides.

# STANCES

# The "Fencer"

The fencing stance (figure 12) used to be advocated by trainers in World Wars I & II. It was thought that if it worked for swordsmen, it should work for knife fighters as well. Unfortunately, they ignored the added protection of range which automatically resulted from the sword's longer length. Knife fighters place themselves in peril when they hold the knife out in front as seen here in figure 12. There is great forward and backward mobility in this stance; however, there is a much greater probability that you will be countered effectively as you close with the enemy.

**Figure 12**

# The "Classic" Military

Figures 13 & 14 demonstrate a much more conservative stance which keeps the knife back out of the range of an enemy's kick, grab, or slash. Weight is evenly distributed and the knife is held back out of the way. The opposite arm is used as a screen and a shield.

"What?", you say. "You want me to leave my arm out in front where it can get cut?" In one word, yes!

If you think you are going to come out of a knife fight completely untouched, you're not being realistic. It's better to take a couple of cuts on your arm if they allow you to counter attack and win.

**Figure 13**

# FIGHTING GRIPS & STANCES

**Figure 14**

This author was talking with the writer of two top notch books on sword and knife making at the 1990 Soldier of Fortune convention in Las Vegas. Before he became a talented blacksmith, he worked as an undercover Drug Enforcement Agency (DEA) agent in the Los Angeles barrios for twelve years.

"Yes," he said. "You're absolutely correct!" He proceeded to hold up a left arm which was crisscrossed with the white lines of knife scars. "I've been in many knife fights to the death as a DEA agent. My arm may be scarred, but I'm still here to tell the story!"

This stance allows good mobility forward, backward, and side-ways. It also gives good stability on uneven terrain.

# The "Hollywooder"

Figure 15 shows the knife being held loosely and out in front in a taunting position. Sometimes this kind of fighter will even toss the knife back and forth from one hand to another in an attempt to dazzle and befuddle his opponent. This is a very weak stance. It brings the knife forward within range of a kick or a slash and demonstrates the lack of meaningful fight experience. The trade off of showing off isn't worth the danger to the knife wielder.

**Figure 15**

# The "Berserker"

The berserker tries to use the combination of a strong grip such as the hammer or ice pick with a totally aggressive, all out attack, driving ever forward. Although not a finesse strategy, it can be dangerously intimidating and effective. The key to countering it is side-ways movement and rapid slashes to the attacker's hand, arm, and legs to slow him down and to take away his strength and speed.

# Ninja style

This is a good stance for surprise attacks. It is mobile in all directions and hides the knife. Its weakness is that it forces the user to lead with his bare hand or arm instead of the blade for most slashing attacks.

# Street Assassin

Figure 16 shows this technique's similarity to the Ninja grip. In this case, one walks past the intended victim (figure 17) and plants the knife backwards in the victim's kidney (figure 18). Then, keep on walking rapidly away from the scene. This works well in crowded urban environments. Its origin is British WWII Hand-to-hand trainer, Captain Fairborne, who had seen it used in Shanghai, China when he was a police officer there.

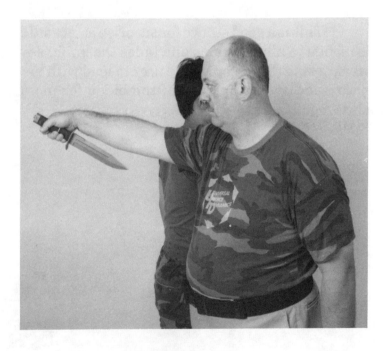

**Figure 16**

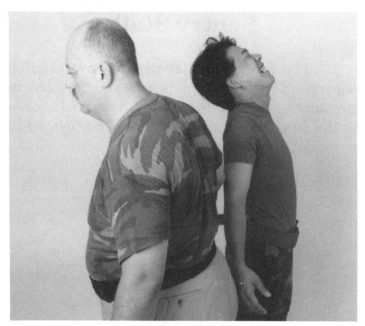

**Figure 17**

**Figure 18**

# Sentry Stalk

Figure 19 shows the proper way to stalk a sentry. The free hand is out and forward in preparation for a grab. The knife is cocked back in anticipation of a thrust. This will be covered in more detail in Chapter 8.

**Figure 19**

# CHAPTER 3

# TARGETS— SECONDARY AND PRIMARY

There's an old saying about the best weapon to bring to a knife fight being a gun. There's a lot to be said for that philosophy; however, you may not always have that luxury. Guns can run out of ammunition. Situations can develop rather quickly on the battlefield when the enemy comes over the wire and starts closing in hand-to-hand combat. If you're forced into a knife fighting situation, it would be wise to know how to use your weapon as well as possible. This chapter addresses the areas of an opponent's body which are most vulnerable to slashes and stabs. They are broken down into two main groups:

- Secondary Targets

- Primary Targets

# MILITARY KNIFE FIGHTING

The two means of attack are slashes and stabbing. Slashes tend to cause a burning sensation and will cause light shock and moderate to heavy loss of blood. Slashes are excellent as counters and follow-on attacks. Stabs tend to hurt much more and cause deep shock as well as having a much greater potential to cause significant harm. They are also more dangerous to execute because they generally require more commitment of movement and body positioning.

## Secondary Targets

Secondary targets are those points which may be attacked to disable or maim. These are generally safer to attack. By attacking them first, you may be able to cause the enemy to surrender. Also, by attacking them first, you may be able to slow him or impede his movements in such a manner as to allow you safer access to the more critical primary targets. The secondary targets are:

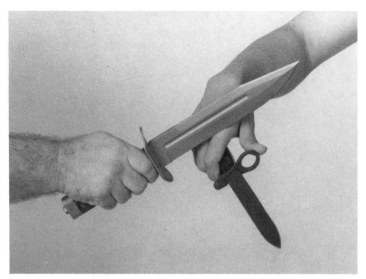

**Figure 1. The fingers / thumb. Cutting these may cause him to drop his knife. At least, his blood will make his grip less sure.**

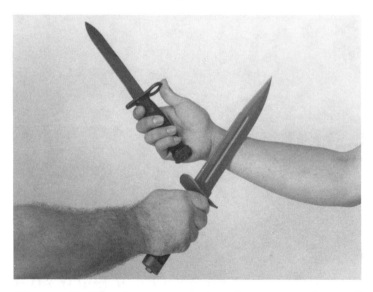

**Figure 2. The inner wrist or forearm. A good chance for an artery or the tendons which control the hand's closing.**

Figure 3. The tendons on the back of the hand. These control the fingers' ability to grip tightly.

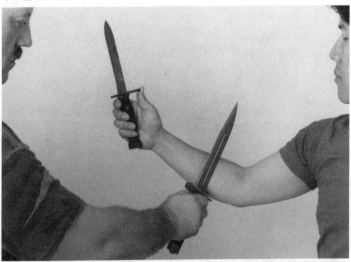

Figure 4. Anywhere on the arm holding the knife. This may cause general weakness of the limb and gives his blood a chance to run down into his grip.

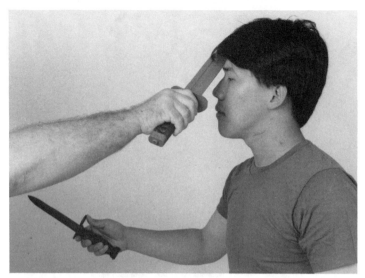

Figure 5. The forehead. Cuts above the eyes will cause stinging, salty blood to run down into the eyes, impairing his vision.

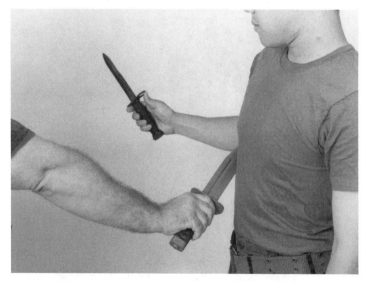

Figure 6. Slashes to the body may have a general weakening effect over time due to shock and blood loss.

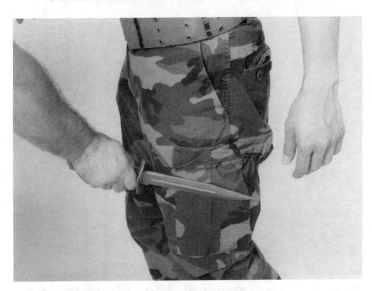

**Figure 7. Slashes to his quadriceps may cripple his leg and slow him down.**

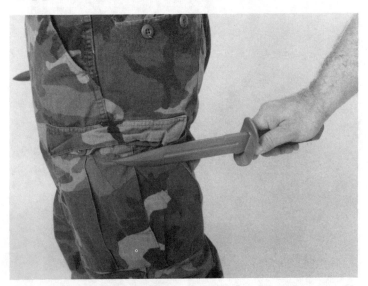

**Figure 8. Slashes to his hamstring tendons can cause his leg to collapse.**

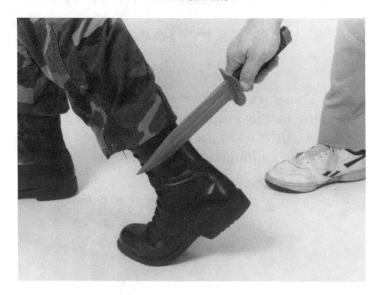

Figure 9. Slashes to his Achilles tendons will cause his foot and leg to collapse.

# MILITARY KNIFE FIGHTING
## Primary Targets

These are target areas which will cause the opponent to die immediately or within a short time, or will cause him to be too injured to fight effectively any longer. They include:

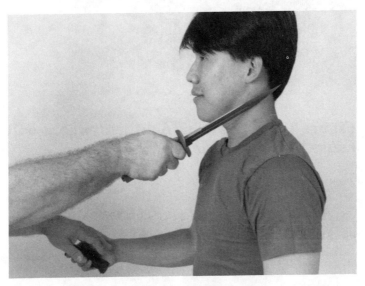

**Figure 10. Slashes or stabs to the throat area.**

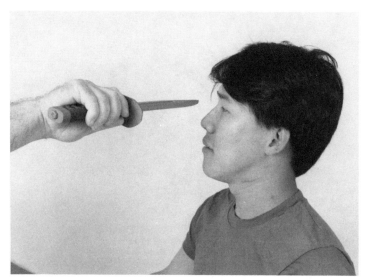

**Figure 11.  Slashes or stabs through or into the eyes.**

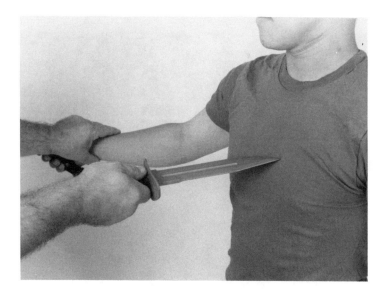

**Figure 12.  Thrusts into the thorax or chest area from front or rear into the heart or lungs.**

# MILITARY KNIFE FIGHTING

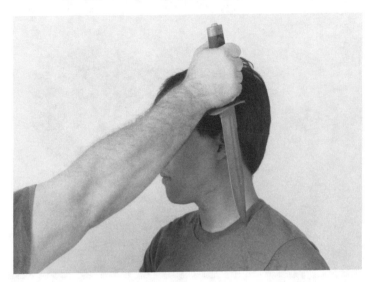

Figure 13. Thrusts downward into the sub-clavian artery area (behind the collar bone and in front of the trapezius muscle).

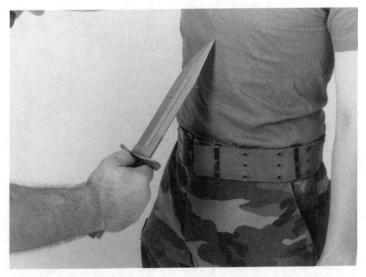

Figure 14. Thrusts into the diaphragm area, angling upward into the heart and lungs.

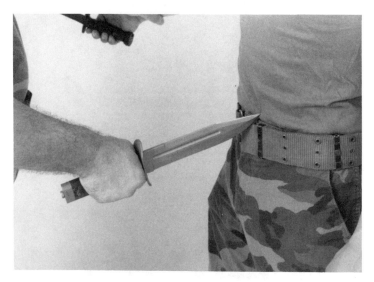

Figure 15. Thrusts into the body cavity's internal organs and intestines.

Figure 16. A deep slash or stab to the femoral artery inside the thigh (a 3-minute bleed-to-death).

# MILITARY KNIFE FIGHTING

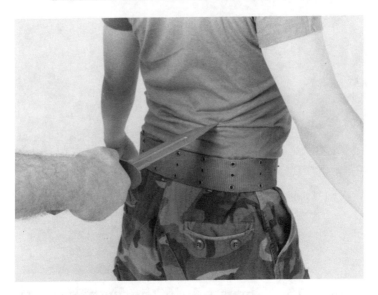

**Figure 17. Thrusts into the kidneys from the side or rear.**

In addition, there are some specific assassination targets which we will cover in more detail in Chapter 8: Sentry Kills.

# CHAPTER 4

# BLOCKS AND COUNTERS

The best way to block an incoming attack from a bladed weapon is to use sharp steel against flesh. The next best method is to use steel against steel. The third method is to block flesh with flesh. The least desirable method is flesh against steel.

We will examine examples of all four methods in this chapter. We will also show how to follow a block with a counter attack. These are merely examples. Once you have the hang of it, you will be able to work out many similar techniques for yourself.

# Steel Against Flesh

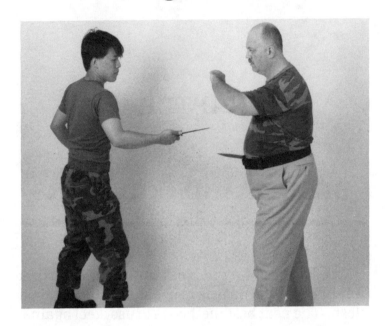

Figure 1. The assailant lunges straight in with a thrust.

**Figure 2.** Block his arm to the outside while you step 45° forward and to your right.

**Figure 3.** Slash across his torso and then retreat.

**Figure 1. The assailant slashes down and across.**

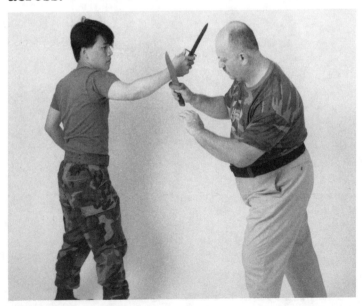

**Figure 2. Block upward, across against his arm or fingers while stepping under his arm.**

**Figure 3. After slicing through his arm, slash his hamstring tendon as you go by.**

Figure 1. The assailant attempts a backhand slash.

Figure 2. Slash his hand tendons or wrist.

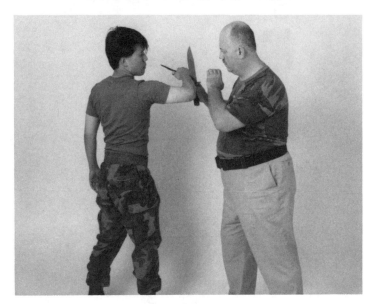

**Figure 3. Continue the circle to slash his quadriceps as you step on by.**

**Figure 1. The assailant attempts a horizontal ninja slash.**

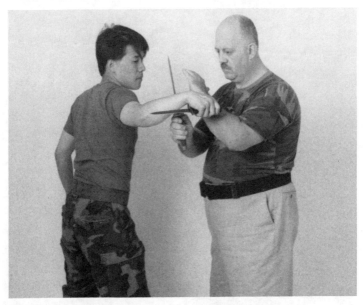

**Figure 2. Step in and slash block his wrist or arm.**

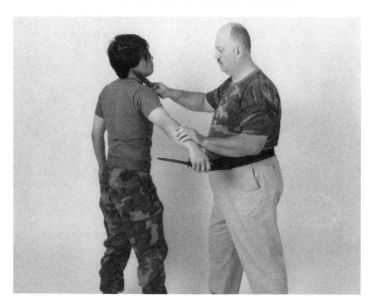

**Figure 3.** Reverse your knife into a throat slash, or a...

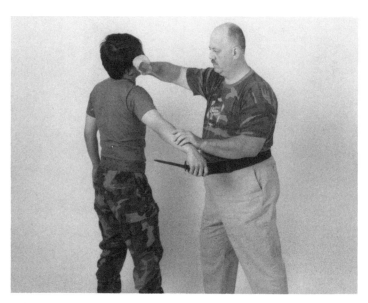

**Figure 4.** Pommel strike to the temple.

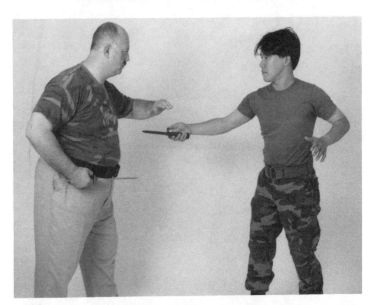

**Figure 1. The assailant tries to plunge his knife into your belly.**

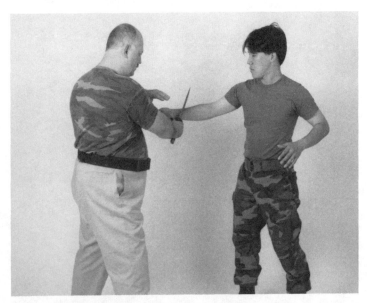

**Figure 2. Step back and slash downward onto his hand.**

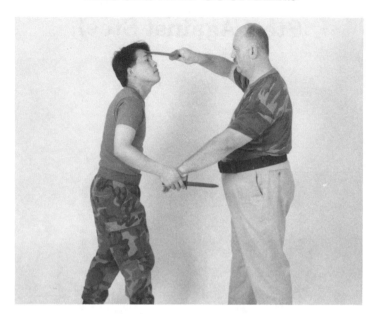

Figure 3.   Slash his forehead or eyes and retreat.

# MILITARY KNIFE FIGHTING
## Steel Against Steel

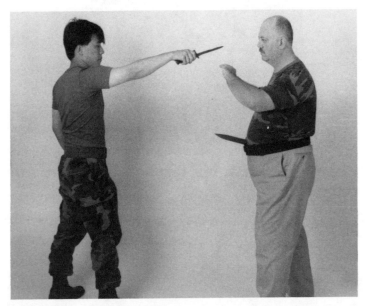

**Figure 1. The assailant thrusts for your eyes.**

# BLOCKS AND COUNTERS

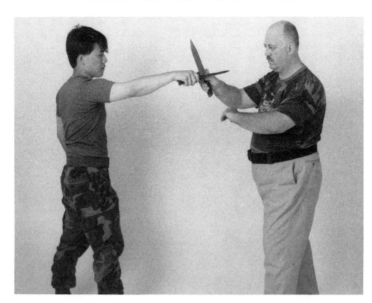

**Figure 2. Meet his blade with yours at the guards.**

**Figure 3. Try to twist your hand so that his knife is wrenched loose from his hand.**

**Figure 1. The assailant attempts a backhand slash.**

**Figure 2. Cross blades at the guard and ...**

**Figure 3. Push him away.**

# Flesh Against Flesh

The primary weapons you should use for countering is the knife edge of your guarding hand or the wrist and forearm bones extending up the arm from the knife edge of the hand. They will generally be used against the assailant's inner wrist tendons. Hard strikes to this area by these weapons can cause temporary paralysis of his arm and hand, and may even cause him to drop his weapon.

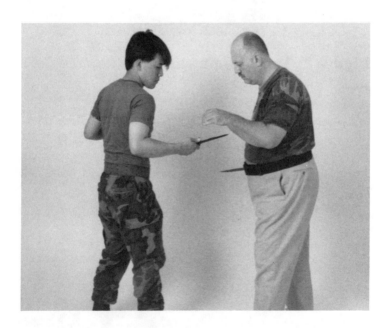

**Figure 1. As the assailant thrusts forward ...**

Figure 2. Step in and block his arm outward while thrusting your own knife forward into his torso.

**Figure 1. As the assailant slashes across.**

**Figure 2. Block outward and stab him in the throat.**

Figure 1. The assailant tries an ice pick stab downward.

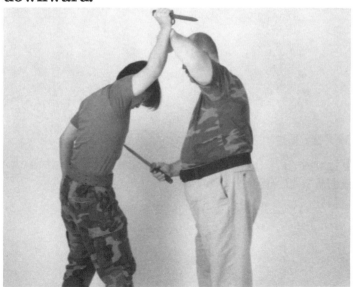

Figure 2. Perform a rising block up under his arm and thrust your knife up into his diaphragm.

# Flesh Against Steel

The least desirable (and therefore the fewest examples), this alternative may be used as a last ditch move. It's for those occasions when there's no time or place for any other alternative.

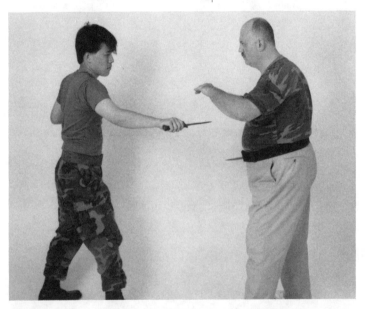

**Figure 1. Your assailant surprise attacks with a thrust.**

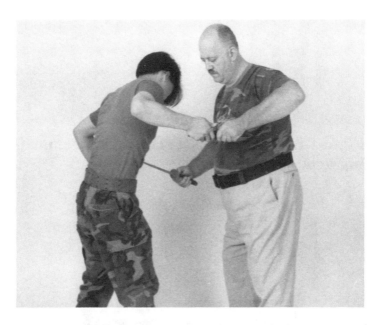

Figure 2. You grab his blade with your hand to prevent it from entering your belly and counter thrust as hard as you can.

# MILITARY KNIFE FIGHTING

**Figure 1. The assailant slashes your guarding arm.**

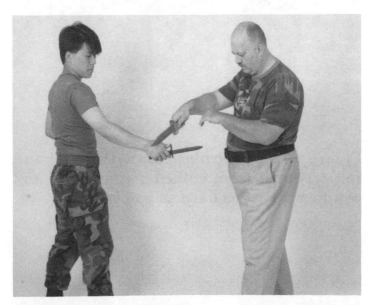

**Figure 2. Try to slash his fingers as he pulls back.**

# CHAPTER 5

# SERIAL ATTACKS

The previous chapter on blocks and counters leads right into this next important concept. Movements, be they blocks, counter attacks, or attacks, should flow from one movement to the next, to the next, and so on. Each movement sets up possibilities for another one. This is what we mean by the terms "Serial Attacks". If you begin to think and practice along these lines, you'll be amazed at how smooth and fast a fighter you can become. It's sort of like a giant chess game. Novice players only think about one move at a time, their next move. Master players think about six moves ahead with all the potential combinations, anticipated reactions, and play / counter plays.

The same goes for really good martial artists with a slight exception. They think ahead at an instinctive level most of the time, instead of thinking consciously. The reason for this is primarily driven by the high speed requirements. It's kind of like excellent racquet ball players who somehow always manage to end up near the ball for their next shot. They know the angles so well, they can anticipate the action just enough to gain an edge. So it is with world class fighters. The neat thing is that it's not that difficult to do in fighting if you train yourself to do it consistently.

This is where Katas or martial art forms tend to fall apart as a training mechanism. Forms are a great way to teach a series of movements to a large audience. They are less effective when it comes to teaching the flow and endless range of possibilities of combat. What does work very well is the use of slow motion walk-throughs of possibilities.

Work with a training partner. Start out by announcing your next move. "Here comes a straight thrust at your belly! (Remember to do it slowly.) What can you do about that?"

Your partner says, "I'm going to block it with my blade and counter with a slash to your torso. What are you going to do about that?

"I'm going to block your slash attempt with my guard arm and knee you in the groin."

Well, you get the idea. You may want to stop from time to time and talk about the relative virtues of other possibilities in the middle of a series of movements. This forces you to look for openings, create your own openings, and begin to develop instincts for tactics and strategy. It definitely enhances combat flow.

Gradually pick up the pace. You'll be amazed how quickly this will improve your skills. Change training partners from time to time so you both don't get too accustomed to one another's moves and styles. This will help you to keep from becoming stale.

This approach to training will also drive home the importance of never making only one movement when three, four, or five can be easily connected. This is a way to think to, through, and beyond your objective. It's great to block a threatening attack. It's much better to block the attack, and get in three counter attacks before your assailant has even realized it. Connecting movements will give you that sense of flow and will pick up your effective speed incredibly. There will be fewer wasted movements and you will be able to use excellent economy of motion. Try especially to walk through moving into and out of the danger zone while making connections with various techniques. This forces you to involve your whole body. Before you know it, openings will begin to appear like magic.

The following illustrations are used simply to give you an idea of how all this works. Remember, there is no single best solution. Fight dynamics are incredibly complex. However, some things work better than others. That's why it's important to train with partners to get fresh viewpoints.

Figure 1. Cut at his hand. Use a rolling wrist motion forward and downward.

Figure 2. You may or may not cut him; however, he will react by drawing his knife back, which sets up the next move.

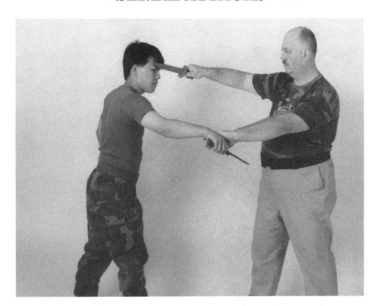

**Figure 3. Try for a forehead slash. He should jerk his head back.**

**Figure 4. Continue your slashing motion down and around toward his knees or legs.**

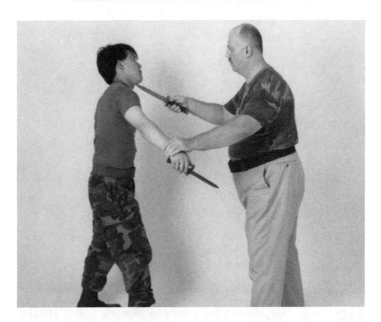

**Figure 5. As he tries to pull his legs back, his upper torso may come forward, giving you a great shot at a thrust for the throat or upper chest area.**


    See how each move set up the next one. Notice also that the opponent was constantly having to react to **you**. You were in control of the fight from the very first move. That's great, keep the pressure on him all the time! It's much easier to remain on the offensive and to keep him reacting.

**Figure 1. Spit in his face, causing him to close his eyes.**

**Figure 2. Follow-up immediately with a stab to the throat.**

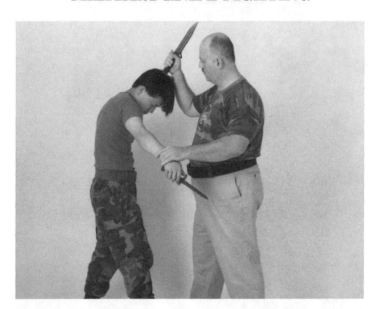

Figure 3. Withdraw and come back around and down for a pommel strike to the top of his head.

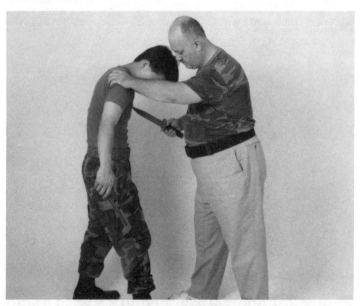

Figure 4. Bury your knife in his heart.

## SERIAL ATTACKS

Are you starting to see the possibilities here? We could give examples all day long, but it will be better if you get out there and start practicing and developing them on your own. **You'll find this type of training to be exciting and fun!**

PARALLEL ATTACKS

# CHAPTER 6

# PARALLEL ATTACKS

Serial attacks mean to make one move after another. Parallel attacks means to make multiple attacks or moves at the same time. Many people tend to forget their whole body can be considered as a weapon. Sometimes, we become fixated on the fact that we have a knife, club, or pistol in our hands. When this happens, we ignore opportunities for exploitation with other means of attacking. For example, I might try to break an opponent's knee with a low side kick while I'm going for a finger cut.

In parallel attacks, I may use my guarding hand to strike at an opponent's face or to grapple with his knife hand while I use my knife against some other target. In other words, use all the weapons in your arsenal. Here are some examples of how this approach might work:

**83**

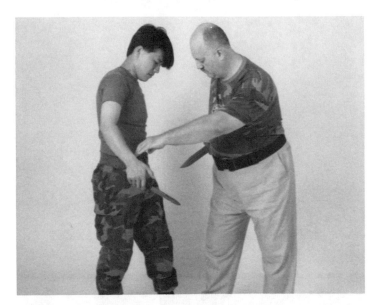

Figure 1. Stomp on your opponent's instep in an attempt to break his foot and to freeze it in place while you ...

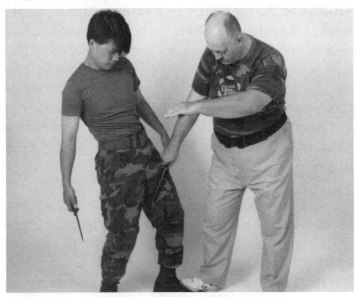

Figure 2.  Slash his femoral artery.

# PARALLEL ATTACKS

Figure 1. Grab his knife arm while you thrust for his body.

Figure 1. Block his backhand slash with your blade, while you try to take out his knee with a stomp kick.

Again, there are thousands of ways in which one can use multiple attacks. Try out a number of them in practice to discover what works best for you.

# CHAPTER 7

# KNIFE GRAPPLING

It has been said that eighty-five percent of all street fights end up on the ground. With the uncertain footing of the battleground, this may also be a common occurrence in hand-to-hand fighting. In fact, some opponents, who may be large and strong, may actively seek this kind of situation. They will quickly close and try to use their superior strength and size in the best manner possible. This chapter addresses the environment of grappling with knives, both when on one's feet and on the ground.

First, the last thing you want to be involved in is a wrestling match. You will want to get your blade free and doing damage to him while you contain his blade. Don't stop trying things until he is past all resistance! The following examples give some insight on how to do that.

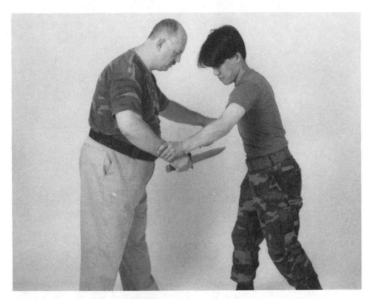

**Figure 1. Both of you tie up while trying to obtain a belly thrust.**

**Figure 2. Don't play strength games! Use your blade to cut free from his grip.**

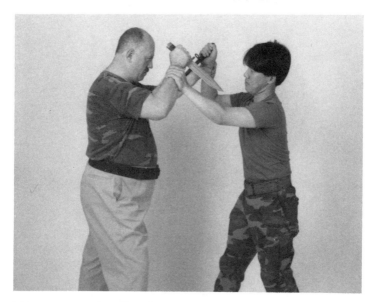

**Figure 1. Both of you tie up while trying to stab one another's chest.**

**Figure 2. Again, cut your way out.**

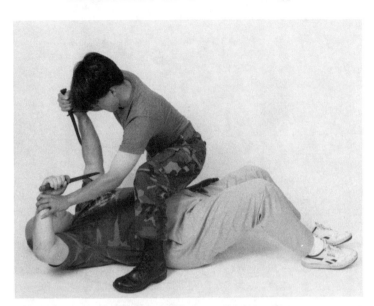

**Figure 1. You're rolling around on the ground and he ends up on top.**

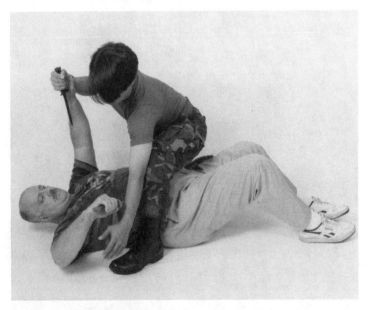

**Figure 2. Cut your way out and go for a ...**

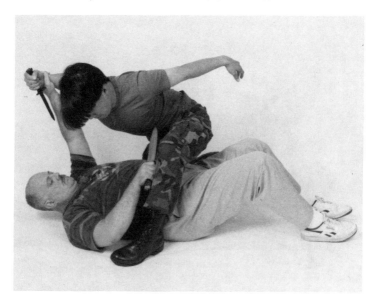

**Figure 3. thrust into his side or back.**

**Figure 1. You're on top.**

**Figure 2.  Use your forehead to butt him in the face as a distractor.**

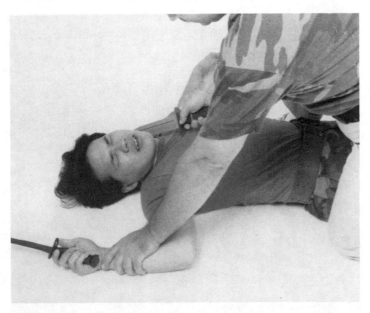

**Figure 3.  Wrench your wrist free and slash his throat.**

# CHAPTER 8

# SENTRY KILLS

The taking out of a sentry without making too much noise is much more difficult than the movies would have you believe. In real life, the sentry is not an actor going by the script which says at this point your character must die. A real sentry is going to fight for his life and fight to get a warning out. Once he hears you or you touch him, he will transform from a man into a raging beast. This means you are going to have to give it your all while still trying to keep the noise level way down. The following techniques are designed to aid you in this; however, they are not fool-proof. Both skill and luck play important roles in sentry neutralizations.

In making your approach, stealthy stalking will be required. This means you should step heel to toe, taking care where your feet go. Don't place them on twigs which might snap. Don't scuff through dead leaves. Slowly and quietly are the watch words. Try to work with the environment, not against it. An excellent way to train for stealth, is to take up bow hunting.

In terms of methods and targets for killing, we are seeking those which help assure silence, provide rapid effect, and minimize the amount of struggle. Figure 1 shows the most vulnerable parts of the head and neck which we will use as targets.

### Figure 1. High Payoff Targets

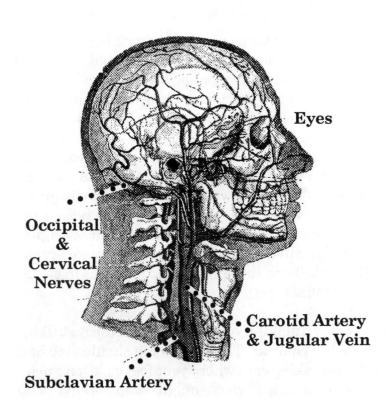

Eyes

Occipital & Cervical Nerves

Carotid Artery & Jugular Vein

Subclavian Artery

**Figure 1.** Clasp his nose and mouth in one hand while thrusting your knife deeply into his kidneys. This will cause him to gasp deeply with sudden shock and pain.

# MILITARY KNIFE FIGHTING

Figure 2. Immediately withdraw your blade from his back and plunge its point deeply into the side of his neck to cut the carotid artery and jugular vein. They will drain into his windpipe, drowning out any screams he might make.

Figure 1. A much messier alternative is to hold the knife in a ninja grip and cut his throat as you come across it. Blood is going to spray all over the place. This is not a recommended method.

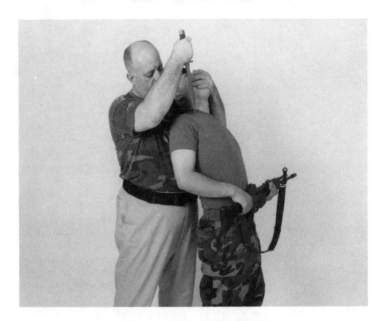

Figure 2. A better way is to stab deeply into the subclavian area and wrench the knife back and forth, seeking to cut the subclavian artery and vein or the aorta of the heart. This will result in rapid loss of blood pressure to the brain.

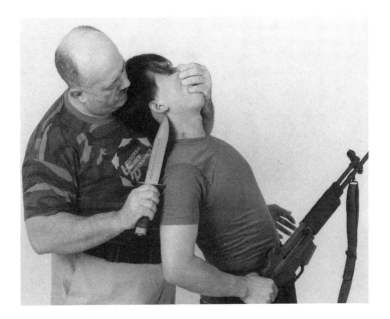

**Figure 3.** Another way is to drive the point of the blade up under the ear into the brain case and wrench the blade back and forth to scramble all the brain connections permanently.

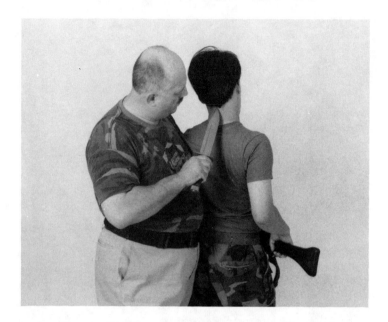

Figure 4. A final way from the rear is to drive the blade point into the base of the skull and wrench it back and forth to sever all the spinal column and brain stem connections.

# SENTRY KILLS

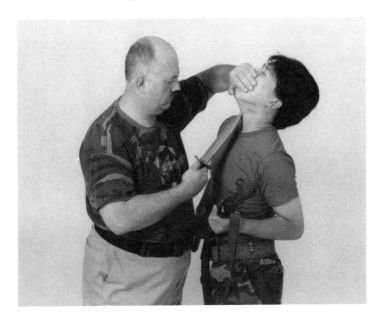

Figure 1. One way from the front is to cover his nose and mouth while ramming the point through the front of his throat. Again, wrench it back and forth for maximum damage. You may have to withdraw the blade and slam it up through his diaphragm into his heart to finish him off.

# CHAPTER 9

# KNIFE VS BAYONET

Nothing is ever fair on the battlefield. The object is to win and live to tell about it. No one is going to say, "Gentlemen, choose your weapons!" People are always going to use the best tools at hand. In a close quarters situation, you might find the only weapon available to you is a knife. What are you going to do if the enemy comes at you with a bayonet on the end of a rifle?

First of all, don't panic. A bayonet is not the most graceful weapon in the world. Most of us who spent hour upon hour practicing its very rudimentary moves and positions in military Basic training can attest to that. The darn thing is just awkward! It is, however, much heavier than a knife. Given that, cheat! Use your guarding arm and hand to help support your counters. Remember, the bayonet and rifle are only as strong as the fingers and hands which are holding them! Here are some techniques you can use. Remember to try to stay fluid and maintain your mobility.

# MILITARY KNIFE FIGHTING

**Figure 1. The assailant begins a long thrust.**

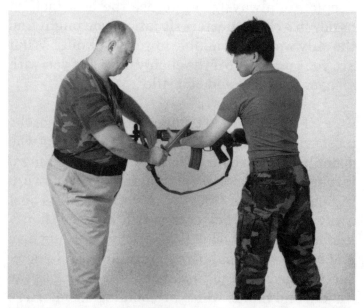

**Figure 2. Step outside its line of attack while slicing at his forward fingers and hand, or...**

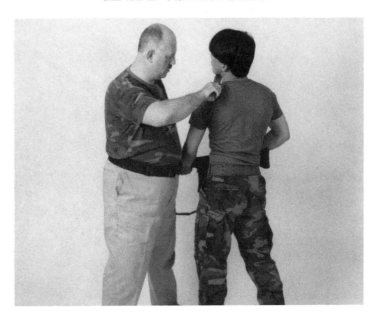

**Figure 3.** Step inside its attack line, pushing it outside with our guard hand and slashing his throat with your knife.

**Figure 1. The assailant attempts a slashing attack.**

**Figure 2. Step inside the line of attack and try to sever his front hand off his arm.**

**Figure 1. The assailant attempts a horizontal butt stroke at your face.**

**Figure 2. Perform a rising block with your guarding forearm, and ...**

# MILITARY KNIFE FIGHTING

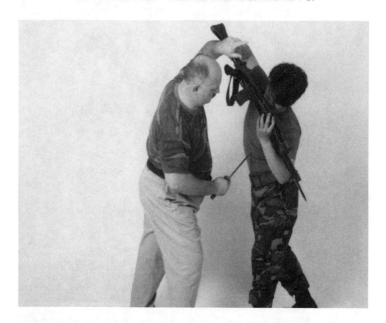

Figure 3.  Bury your knife in his belly.

# CHAPTER 10

# KNIFE VS ENTRENCHING TOOL

"Why would he write a chapter on that?", you may wonder. Well, after conducting research on foreign armies, I discovered at least two major potential foes (plus all their surrogate forces) train extensively with the entrenching tool (fold-up camp shovel) as a weapon. The Soviet airborne forces sharpen the edges of their shovels and practice throwing them and using them on a bayonet assault course.

The North Koreans have even developed Katas for the entrenching tool. I have seen movies of them in training. These two threat armies train more Third World forces and terrorists than any other nation.

"Ah so," you say. "Now I understand!"

Yes, its a real threat. The entrenching tool can be a formidable weapon. U.S. Medal of Honor winner, Master Sergeant Benjamin F. Wilson, killed four enemy soldiers on June 5, 1951, near Hwa Chon Myon, Korea, with one.

In fact, this weapon presents a much more dangerous threat to a knife fighter than does a bayonet. The entrenching tool is shorter, lighter, and much more maneuverable than the bayonet. It's similar to an Aztec or Mayan war club.

Do not attempt to block the entrenching tool with your arm or knife. It will blow right through puny defenses such as these. You're going to have to try to out-maneuver your opponent and get way far away or get inside where he can't hurt you as much as you can hurt him.

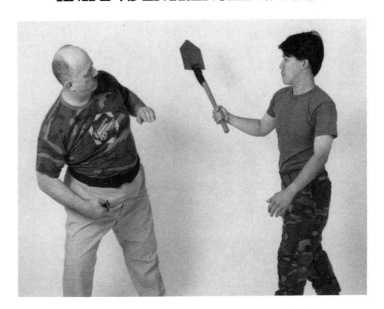

**Figure 1. Try to lean back out of the way, then ...**

**Figure 2. Close in as it goes by.**

**Figure 1. If he swings at you horizontally, ...**

**Figure 2. Try to step inside the swing.**

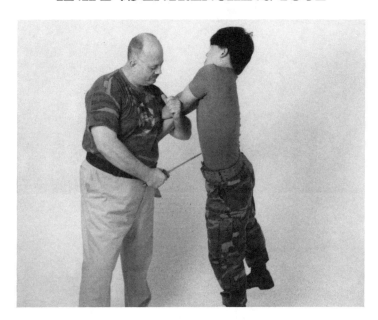

**Figure 3.** Grab his arms with your guarding arm and knife the heck out of him. You don't dare play games with this character.

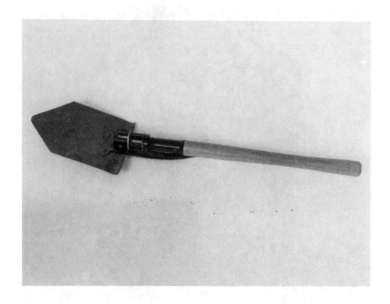

A potentially lethal weapon, the entrenching tool.

# CHAPTER 11

# KNIFE THROWING

I think most of us have heard a Drill Sergeant say, "Never throw your knife! It's a cowboy stunt and just too uncertain." And, he is absolutely right, with one exception. What if the enemy is standing twenty feet away? What if he's getting ready to shoot your sorry self and you've just run out of ammo? What if all you have is your knife?

In that case, what the heck? You might as well throw it at him. Maybe it will help buy you some time or give you an edge (sorry for the pun). He may flinch or blink. Who knows, you might even be lucky enough to stick it in him.

For these reasons, I will address this subject briefly, even though whole books have been dedicated to knife throwing. As I mentioned in the Foreword, I've been throwing knives for a very long time. Though I have occasionally been fairly good with one, in general, knife throwing is usually pretty inconsistent. This is why Drill Sergeants make the statements they do.

There are two ways one can throw a knife, by its handle, or by its blade. If you throw it by the handle, it will stick whenever the knife makes full revolutions. For example, it will stick on the first, second, third, and so on revolutions. If you throw it by the blade, it will stick on the half revolutions, such as 1/2, 1 1/2, 2 1/2, etc. All you have to guess is how many exact revolutions it is to the target.

Weapon balance plays a role in this as well. It is better to hold it by its lightest end, since that will give the throw more force. The Field Fighter throws best from its handle. My Gerber Mark II throws best from its blade. If the knife is truly balanced in the middle, it doesn't matter so much.

The way one throws it is also important, because that can control the spin speed of the knife. All throws are best done with an overhand pitch. If you stiff-arm the throw, the spin will be very slow. If you add lots of wrist motion to it, the spin will be very fast. The manner in which the knife is held is also important. If you hold it at the tip, it will spin faster. If you choke up on it and hold more of the knife, it will spin slower. So, what should you do? It depends on the knife, the distance, and the situation. This requires thousands of hours of practice to consistently guess the exact right combination of techniques for a given distance. When the exact distance is unknown, and the situation is Panic City, it's going to be darn hard to be right on the money with the spin. For instance, I can stand at a distance, say three meters, and consistently stick the point using several combinations of these throwing technique variations. But, then I knew the exact distance. If I don't and I'm real rushed, sticking the knife becomes pure luck.

There is one consolation. If this is a battlefield situation and you're going for broke anyway, aim the throw for the base of his throat. If the points sticks, you're going to ruin his whole day. If the knife butt strikes, it may crush his larynx. If the flat of the blade strikes, it certainly can be a distractor. What have you got to lose?

# MILITARY KNIFE FIGHTING

## Figures 1&2.  A stiff-armed throw

# KNIFE THROWING

**Figures 3&4.  A wrist flip throw.**

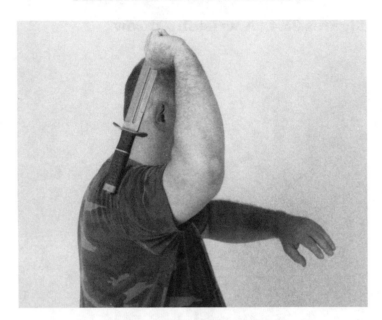

**Figure 5. Holding at the tip.**

**Figure 6. Choking up.**

# CHAPTER 12

# TRAINING HINTS

Well, we've pretty much covered the waterfront in terms of type threats and fighting approaches. Now it's time to put them to use in your practice sessions. Here are some suggestions which may make your training more meaningful:

• Practice safety first; however, don't be afraid to use wooden training knives for realism.
• Train with partners or groups for variety.
• Talk through possibilities and rehearse them. Try to always think in terms of combination moves.
• Start slowly, then gradually pick up the training speed. Walk before you run.
• Constantly seek additional applications of the theories addressed in this book.
• Practice with unequal weapon types to better prepare for reality.
• Try fighting in a melee of numerous people and different types of weapons.

# MILITARY KNIFE FIGHTING

One source of interesting practice I have discovered recently is the Society for Creative Anachronism (the S.C.A.). This is an interesting bunch of medieval recreationists who don metal and leather armor and flail away at one another with rattan weapons. It sounds hokey, but it makes for some very serious stuff. Although rattan is bulkier, it has about the same weight as an equivalent length of steel weaponry. The stuff bruises, even through the armor. Their fighting activities will teach you a respect for edged weapons more than anything I know. It is really interesting to discover how hard it is to fight in full armor on a hot day.

These people are fanatical about their sport /art. They even travel thousands of miles to participate in wars with several thousand people on a side. I have served as a fight coach to the Baron of our local shire for the past year and a half, and have found this to be a real eye opener. It's interesting that the only way one can become King of a Regional Kingdom, is by winning its Crown Tournament. These people practice what they preach. You might try it for kicks. Local baronies can usually be found around most large college campuses. For further information contact:

**The Office of the Registry**
**Society for Creative Anachronism, Inc.**
**P.O. Box 360743**
**Milpitas, CA 95035-0743**
**(408) 263-9305, M-Th, 9:30 AM - 4:00 PM**
**Pacific Time**

# INQUIRIES

Mr. Spear is available for consultation on training programs, weapon design, or as an expert witness specializing in appropriate levels of force cases.

Inquiries may be made directly through this publishing house.  Contact:

**Universal Force Dynamics Publishing**
**Attn:  Barbara Sharp, Customer Relations**
**410 Delaware**
**Leavenworth, KS  66048**
**(913) 682-6518**

# Notes

# Other Books Available From Desert Publications

| No. | Title | Price |
|---|---|---|
| 001 | Firearms Silencers Volume 1 | $9.95 |
| 003 | The Silencer Cookbook | $9.95 |
| 004 | Select Fire Uzi Modification Manual | $9.95 |
| 005 | Expedient Hand Grenades | $16.95 |
| 007 | 007 Travel Kit, The | $8.00 |
| 008 | Law Enforcement Guide to Firearms Silencer | $8.95 |
| 009 | Springfield Rifle, The | $11.95 |
| 010 | Full Auto Vol 3 MAC-10 Mod Manual | $9.95 |
| 012 | Fighting Garand, The | $11.95 |
| 013 | M1 Carbine Owners Manual | $9.95 |
| 014 | Ruger Carbine Cookbook | $11.95 |
| 015 | M-14 Rifle, The | $9.95 |
| 016 | AR-15, M16 and M16A1 5.56mm Rifles | $11.95 |
| 017 | Shotguns | $11.95 |
| 019 | AR15 A2/M16A2 Assault Rifle | $8.95 |
| 022 | Full Auto Vol 7 Bingham AK-22 | $9.95 |
| 025 | Full Auto Vol 4 Thompson SMG | $9.95 |
| 030 | STANAG Mil-Talk | $9.95 |
| 031 | Thompson Submachine Guns | $13.95 |
| 033 | H&R Reising Submachine Gun Manual | $12.95 |
| 035 | How to Build Silencers | $6.95 |
| 036 | Full Auto Vol 2 Uzi Mod Manual | $9.95 |
| 049 | Firearm Silencers Vol 3 | $13.95 |
| 050 | Firearm Silencers Vol 2 | $19.95 |
| 054 | Company Officers HB of Ger. Army | $11.95 |
| 056 | German Infantry Weapons Vol 1 | $14.95 |
| 058 | Survival Armory | $27.95 |
| 060 | Survival Gunsmithing | $9.95 |
| 061 | FullAuto Vol 1 Ar-15 Mod Manual | $8.95 |
| 064 | HK Assault Rifle Systems | $7.95 |
| 065 | SKS Type of Carbines, The | $16.95 |
| 066 | Private Weaponeer, The | $9.95 |
| 067 | Rough Riders, The | $24.95 |
| 068 | Lasers & Night Vision Devices | $9.95 |
| 069 | Ruger P-85 Family of Handguns | $11.95 |
| 071 | Dirty Fighting | $11.95 |
| 072 | Live to Spend It | $29.95 |
| 073 | Military Ground Rappelling Techniques | $11.95 |
| 074 | Smith & Wesson Autos | $7.95 |
| 080 | German MG-34 Machinegun Manual | $9.95 |
| 081 | Crossbows/ From 35 Years With the Weapon | $11.95 |
| 082 | Op. Man. 7.62mm M24 Sniper Weapon | $7.95 |
| 083 | USMC AR-15/M-16 A2 Manual | $16.95 |
| 084 | Urban Combat | $21.95 |
| 085 | Caching Techniques of U.S. Army Special Forces | $9.95 |
| 086 | US Marine Corps Essential Subjects | $16.95 |
| 087 | The L I M-1, The .30 Cal. M-1 Carbine | $14.95 |
| 088 | Concealed Carry Made Easy | $9.95 |
| 089 | Apocalypse Tomorrow | $17.95 |
| 090 | M14 and M14A1 Rifles and Rifle Marksmanship | $16.95 |
| 091 | Crossbow As a Modern Weapon | $11.95 |
| 092 | MP40 Machinegun | $11.95 |
| 093 | Map Reading and Land Navigation | $19.95 |
| 094 | U. S. Marine Corps Scout/Sniper Training Manual | $16.95 |
| 095 | Clear Your Record & Own a Gun | $14.95 |
| 096 | Sig Handguns | $9.95 |
| 097 | Poor Man's Nuclear Bomb | $19.95 |
| 098 | Poor Man's Sniper Rifle | $14.95 |
| 100 | Submachine Gun Designers Handbook | $16.95 |
| 101 | Lock Picking Simplified | $8.50 |
| 102 | Combination Lock Principles | $8.95 |
| 103 | How to Fit Keys by Impressioning | $7.95 |
| 104 | Keys To Understanding Tubular Locks | $9.95 |
| 105 | Techniques of Safe & Vault Manipulation | $9.95 |
| 106 | Lockout - Techniques of Forced Entr | $11.95 |
| 107 | Bugs Electronic Surveillance | $11.95 |
| 110 | Improvised Weapons of Amer. Undergrnd | $10.00 |
| 111 | Training Handbook of the American Underground | $10.00 |
| 114 | FullAuto Vol 8 M14A1 & Mini 14 | $9.95 |
| 116 | Handbook Bomb Threat/Search Procedures | $8.00 |
| 117 | Improvised Lock Picks | $10.00 |
| 119 | Fitting Keys By Reading Locks | $7.00 |
| 120 | How To Open Handcuffs Without Keys | $9.95 |
| 121 | Electronic Locks Volume 1 | $8.00 |
| 122 | With British Snipers, To the Reich | $24.95 |
| 125 | Browning Hi-Power Pistols | $9.95 |
| 126 | P-08 Parabellum Luger Auto Pistol | $9.95 |
| 127 | Walther P-38 Pistol Manual | $9.95 |
| 128 | Colt .45 Auto Pistol | $9.95 |
| 129 | Beretta - 9MM M9 | $11.95 |
| 130 | FullAuto Vol 5 M1 Carbine to M2 | $9.95 |
| 132 | Ranger Handbook | $16.95 |
| 133 | FN-FAL Auto Rifles | $13.95 |
| 135 | AK-47 Assault Rifle | $11.95 |
| 136 | UZI Submachine Gun | $9.95 |
| 139 | USMC Battle Skills Training Manual | $24.95 |
| 140 | Sten Submachine Gun, The | $9.95 |
| 141 | Terrorist Explosives Handbook | $6.95 |
| 142 | U. S. Army Counterterrorism Training Manual | $14.95 |
| 143 | Sniper Training | $24.95 |
| 144 | The Butane Lighter Handgrenade | $12.95 |
| 146 | The Official Makarov Pistol Manual | $12.95 |
| 147 | Official Makarov 9mm Pistol Manual | $12.95 |
| 148 | Unarmed Against the Knife | $9.95 |
| 149 | Black book of Booby Traps | $14.95 |
| 151 | Militia Battle Manual | $9.95 |
| 152 | Glock's Handguns | $17.95 |
| 153 | Heckler and Koch's Handguns | $17.95 |
| 154 | The Poor Man's R. P. G. | $14.95 |
| 155 | The Poor Man's Ray Gun | $9.95 |
| 156 | The Anachist Handbook Vol. 2 | $11.95 |
| 157 | How to Make Disposable Silencers Vol. 2 | $16.95 |

| No. | Title | Price |
|---|---|---|
| 158 | Modern Day Ninjutsu | $14.95 |
| 159 | The Squeaky Wheel | $12.95 |
| 160 | The Sicilian Blade | $13.95 |
| 162 | The Anarchist Handbook Vol. 1 | $11.95 |
| 163 | How to Make Disposable Silencers Vol. 1 | $16.95 |
| 164 | The Anarchist Handbook Vol. 3 | $11.95 |
| 165 | How to Build Practical Firearm Silencers | $11.95 |
| 200 | Fighting Back on the Job | $11.95 |
| 202 | Secret Codes & Ciphers | $9.95 |
| 204 | Improvised Munitions Black Book Vol 1 | $14.95 |
| 205 | Improvised Munitions Black Book Vol 2 | $14.95 |
| 206 | CIA Field Exp. Preparation of Black Powder | $8.95 |
| 207 | CIA Field Exp. Meth/Explo. Preparat | $8.95 |
| 209 | CIA Improvised Sabotage Devices | $12.00 |
| 210 | CIA Field Exp. Incendiary Manual | $12.00 |
| 211 | Science of Revolutionary Warfare | $9.95 |
| 212 | Agents HB of Black Bag Ops. | $9.95 |
| 214 | Electronic Harassment | $11.95 |
| 217 | Improvised Rocket Motors | |
| 218 | Impro. Munitions/Ammonium Nitrate | $9.95 |
| 219 | Improvised Batteries/Det. Devices | $8.95 |
| 220 | Impro. Explo/Use In Deton. Devices | $7.95 |
| 221 | Evaluation of Imp Shaped Charges | $8.95 |
| 222 | American Tools of Intrigue | $12.00 |
| 225 | Impro. Munitions Black Book Vol 3 | $23.95 |
| 226 | Poor Man's James Bond Vol 2 | $24.95 |
| 227 | Explosives and Propellants | $11.95 |
| 229 | Select Fire 10/22 | $11.95 |
| 230 | Poor Man's James Bond Vol 1 | $24.95 |
| 231 | Assorted Nasties | $19.95 |
| 232 | Full Auto Modification Manual | $18.95 |
| 234 | L.A.W. Rocket System | $8.00 |
| 240 | Clandestine Ops Man/Central America | $11.95 |
| 241 | Mercenary Operations Manual | $9.95 |
| 250 | Improvised Shaped Charges | $8.95 |
| 251 | Two Component High Exp. Mixtures | $9.95 |
| 260 | Survival Evasion & Escape | $9.95 |
| 262 | Infantry Scouting, Patrol & Sniping | $11.95 |
| 263 | Engineer Explosives of WWI | $7.95 |
| 300 | Brown's Alcohol Motor Fuel Cookbook | $13.95 |
| 301 | How to Build a Junkyard Still | $11.95 |
| 303 | Alcohol Distillers Handbook | $17.95 |
| 306 | Brown's Book of Carburetors | $11.95 |
| 310 | MAC-10 Cookbook | $9.95 |
| 350 | Cheating At Cards | $12.00 |
| 400 | Brown's Lawsuit Cookbook | $18.95 |
| 401 | Hand to Hand Combat | $11.95 |
| 402 | USMC Hand to Hand Combat | $7.95 |
| 403 | US Marine Bayonet Training | $8.95 |
| 404 | Camouflage | $9.95 |
| 409 | Guide to Germ Warfare | $13.95 |
| 410 | Emergency War Surgery | $24.95 |
| 411 | Homeopathic First Aid | $9.95 |
| 412 | Defensive Shotgun | $12.95 |
| 414 | Hand to Hand Combat by D'Eliscue | $7.95 |
| 415 | 999 Survived | $6.00 |
| 416 | Sun, Sand & Survival | $6.00 |
| 420 | USMC Sniping | $13.95 |
| 424 | Prisons Bloody Iron | $15.95 |
| 425 | Napoleon's Maxims of War | $8.95 |
| 432 | Invisible Weapons/Modern Ninja | $11.95 |
| 435 | Cold Weather Survival | $11.95 |
| 436 | Homestead Carpentry | $10.00 |
| 437 | Construction Secret Hiding Places | $11.95 |
| 438 | US Army Survival | $29.95 |
| 439 | Survival Shooting for Women | $11.95 |
| 440 | Survival Medicine | $7.95 |
| 442 | Can You Survive | $12.95 |
| 443 | Canteen Cup Cookery | $9.95 |
| 444 | Leadership Hanbook of Small Unit Ops | $11.95 |
| 445 | Vigilante Handbook | $11.95 |
| 447 | Shootout II | $14.95 |
| 448 | Catalog of Military Suppliers | $14.95 |
| 453 | Survival Childbirth | $8.95 |
| 454 | Police Karate | $10.95 |
| 456 | Survival Guns | $21.95 |
| 457 | Water Survival Training | $5.95 |
| 470 | Emergency Medical Care/Disaster | $11.95 |
| 502 | Guerilla Warfare | $14.95 |
| 504 | Ranger Training & Operations | $14.95 |
| 507 | Spec. Forces Demolitions Trng HB | $16.95 |
| 510 | Battlefield Analysis/Inf. Weapons | $9.95 |
| 512 | US Army Bayonet Training | $7.95 |
| 542 | Desert Storm Weap. Recog. Guide | $9.95 |
| 544 | Professional Homemade Cher Bomb | $10.95 |
| 551 | Combat Loads for Sniper Rifles | $12.00 |
| 552 | Take My Gun. If You Dare | $10.95 |
| 610 | Aunt Bessie's Wood Stove Cookbook | $7.50 |
| C-002 | Trapping & Destruc. of Exec. Cars | $10.00 |
| C-011 | How To Open a Swiss Bank Account | $6.95 |
| C-020 | Defending Your Retreat | $9.95 |
| C-023 | Methods Of Long Term Storage | $8.95 |
| C-029 | Federal Firearms Laws | $4.50 |
| C-038 | M1 Carbine Arsenal History | $6.95 |
| C-040 | Hw To Build A Beer Can Morter | $4.95 |
| C-050 | Criminal Use of False ID | $11.95 |
| C-052 | Surviving Doomsday | $11.95 |
| C-175 | CIA Explosives for Sabotage | $9.00 |
| C-386 | Beat the Box | $7.95 |
| C-679 | Self-Defense Requires No Apology | $11.95 |
| FP-9 | M16A1 Rifle Manual Cartoon Version | $6.95 |
| | Micro Uzi Select Fire Mod Manual | $9.95 |

PRICES SUBJECT TO CHANGE WITHOUT NOTICE

**DESERT Publications**
P.O. Box 1751 Dept. BK-179
El Dorado, AR 71730-1751 USA

501-862-2077    $5.95 shipping & handling